ONE A DAY
SPIRITUAL WARFARE

For more books by Bill Mallory
https://billmallorybooks.com

ONE A DAY
SPIRITUAL WARFARE

BILL MALLORY

W O R K B O O K

REDEMPTION
PRESS

Published by Redemption Press, PO Box 427, Enumclaw, WA 98022.

ISBN 13: 978-1-63232-927-1
Library of Congress Catalog Card Number: 2009902134

CONTENTS

Read the text and write the answers to the questions in the workbook.

INTRODUCTION

OUR CONGREGATION HAD a terrible time trying to hold things together after each different spiritual attack. We would build up to around 100 people, then the attack would come. The twenty or so people that were left would pick up the pieces as best we could, get another pastor and hope for the best. What we didn't know was where the problem actually originated. We were putting a natural bandage on a spiritual problem. The enemy knew that if he could just get the pastor into trouble, the congregation would suffer as well.

1. Have you ever noticed some kind of dominant spirit in one location that differs from other locations?

2. Are there rampant crime and predominant problems over that area?

3. Is there a history of specific problems that are still evident today?

4. Does an area seem to have specific things happening throughout?

5. Could there be a ruling demon over that area?

6. Can you identify underlying attitudes and problems where you live now?

NOTES

WHAT A PREDICAMENT

Chapter 1

THE VERY FIRST ELECTION

PRIDE IS A very destructive force. It was Satan's downfall and he still uses it against God's people today. He knows pride can separate, so he pumps it up on the Earth. God knows how to deal with pride and is very conclusive about it. God has shown His power through creation and He has given us a way to come to Him.

We can come to Him in spite of the devil's wily ways.

1. Who was the most beautiful angel in heaven?

2. What was his attitude?

3. What did he do to try to be the Most High God?

4. Did he win or lose?

5. What did God do to him?

6. Where did he go and what was his plan?

7. What was God's recourse?

8. Who does God use to combat the devil?

9. What has God given the church to help us learn to cooperate with Him in this conflict?

NOTES

Chapter 2

WHERE IS THE WAR?

I WAS TALKING to a guy who said there isn't any spiritual war going on. I think he just believes people are either good or bad with no outer influence. However, natural eyes are not enough to see the supernatural. It's easy to blame what you see or rationalize the problem, then believe the rationalization. The devil whispers, "See those people? They are the problem," when all the time the devil is lying and pitting one against another.

1. Where is the war?

2. Who is stirring up the war?

3. Why do we usually look for someone to blame when there is trouble?

4. Why is it easier for us to believe a lie than to believe the truth?

5. When you have negative ideas and attitudes interjected into your thinking about people or situations, could these be a bombardment by Satan?

6. Who is Satan trying to be when he manipulates like that?

7. What evidence is there of the enemy's activity in nations and governments?

8. Does it seem like there is more trouble on the earth now than during previous centuries?

NOTES

Chapter 3

WE ARE BORN IN THE MIDDLE OF A WAR

BABIES AREN'T VERY smart when they are born; they have to learn everything. When we are born into the Kingdom of God the same thing is true, except now we have a helper inside of us. The time span in between is tough. We think we learn this or that only to find out something's wrong. We are surrounded by truths, half truths and believable lies, which send our conscience spinning. The logical side of our brain is trying to figure all this out and make a straight science out of it. When we finally decide on a particular worldview, something comes along to shake it up. So we put our head in our hands and say, "What is real?"

1. Whose side were you on when you were born?

2. Why does the Christian life always seem so difficult?

3. Where does all the condemnation come from?

4. Why is peace so fleeting?

5. Why don't things make us happy?

6. Can we change our luck?

7. Look around: is God losing the war?

NOTES

Chapter 4

WILLY AND THE ANGEL

MY GOOD FRIEND, Willy, is a great cook and loves to fish. One time, he made me a couple of Ooligan Oil eagle bowls. Never tried Ooligan oil though—I understand it is fermented herring oil for dipping fish in. Anyway, I really believed his story because that is the way angels are. They are sent to help those who will be saved.

How big are angels? This one was awesome enough to scare the gang away.

1. Do you think Willy was set up for this scene?

2. What did they think about spiritual warfare when they bought the beer?

3. What did they think about spiritual warfare after the fight?

4. Why did the angel help them?

5. Will angels help you?

6. Willy used beer cans to fight the enemy. What did God use?

7. Which method was more effective—man's or God's?

8. Since Willy became a Christian after this experience, who do you think initiated his move to Christ?

9. Was this a spiritual battle?

10. Can we expect angels to help us?

NOTES

Chapter 5

HOW BIG IS THE BATTLE?

EVERYONE'S WORLD IS a different size. I work with some physically blind people whose world is smaller than mine. I can see. I can hear. I've been to other countries. I can read the headlines. I'm older than they are so I have seen and heard more. Studying spiritual warfare has given me a much bigger view.

The war we are waging is worldwide and bigger than any one of us can handle. But it's not too big for God.

1. Do you ever feel that you have enough problems of your own and you don't want to think about anyone else's?

2. Does it give you hope to know that God is with you and He will help you?

3. What is a simple way to figure out how big the battle is?

4. If the task is as overwhelming as it seems, how can we accomplish it?

5. Where do you think your segment of the battle is?

6. Are you engaging in battle in those areas?

7. Who must we depend upon for help?

8. How can we help those on the other side of the world?

<u>NOTES</u>

Chapter 6

THE BATTLE WITHIN AND WITHOUT

THERE HAVE BEEN times in my life that I just didn't know. I didn't know who I really was. I didn't know what I was supposed to do. I didn't know about the battle going on overhead for my soul. Life is so tricky and fragile that if I don't get constant counseling from the Lord I tend to wander and squander.

Fortunately I live in a country that has fairly decent standards so I can live comfortably and peacefully—praise the Lord! But I can imagine many countries are in constant confusion, so you can't even find out who you are. Our freedom of worship is awesome and allows a person easy access to the Almighty God through Christ for salvation.

There are many diversions in affluence that hinder a person from coming to Christ. But through the hard times the Lord is accessible; He is but a prayer away.

1. Why is this life and the spiritual battle so confusing?

2. Can't we just figure it out and do it right?

3. Does the truth have dominance in depressed areas?

4. What part of culture is in the battle zone?

5. Does culture need to be sophisticated to have peace?

6. Does lawfulness in the land change the nature of the spiritual war?

7. And how does it change the war?

8. How can we have peace inside when there is war outside?

9. Is there a way we can wage war and win when things are going wrong around us?

NOTES

Chapter 7

THE ANCIENT BATTLE

I GET HAPPY when I meet somebody new and responsive. I can tell them all of my jokes, hoping they haven't heard any of them. I don't learn many new jokes so I must rely on my old ones. Beyond that I just wing it.

I have a feeling that the devil uses similar tactics in that he plays his old tricks on humans. "The old ones worked well; let's try them again." Experience shows us the trend of his tricks so we can be aware and come against them.

Experience gained when reading the Bible helps us to know when the Lord or someone else is talking.

Another thing I have noticed is that the devil is not creative. I don't believe he is as creative as humans are, so it is smart not to give him any evil ideas. Whether it is a written murder mystery, a TV program, or an evil word spoken, the enemy is open to suggestions.

The three monkeys apply here: See no evil, Hear no evil, and Speak no evil. Can you see them with their hands covering their eyes, ears, and mouth? I think this is a good plan.

1. When did this battle start?

2. Is the enemy using new tricks?

3. Why is the enemy so determined to hurt us?

4. How is God able to outsmart the devil?

5. Can the devil get the upper hand on God?

6. How does the devil capitalize on man's forgetfulness?

7. What do we learn from mankind's history?

8. How can you choose not to fight in the battle?

9. How does God woo people into His kingdom?

10. How does Satan woo people into his kingdom?

11. Can you think of an area of your life where the devil tries to trick you and lead you away from God?

12. Do you want to see that change? Can you think of some practical steps you can take to turn that weakness into strength?

NOTES

Chapter 8

WHERE THERE'S SMOKE THERE'S FIRE

WHEN YOU START to do something or say something and you sense a check in your spirit, what happens? Does your spirit or the Holy Spirit say, "Don't go there."? I figure this is being led by peace. I try to obey these signals rather than find out later that they would have kept me from a place that I shouldn't have gone.

It is better to learn from others' mistakes or from the Bible, rather than from our own experience. When we have experiences they quickly become a lasting part of our soul. It is a hard process to get rid of them, especially if we find out later that they don't belong in our lives. In addition, the enemy is taking notes and will try to harass us with guilt.

We should quickly receive our Father's discipline that keeps us away from the blind alleys of despair and self-condemnation. God can help us by giving us His power to walk with wisdom and discretion.

1. What are the signs that signal something is wrong?

2. How can we make our response to a situation better or worse?

3. In all the smoke, how can we find our way?

4. Who is doing the condemning if we feel condemned?

5. How does the Holy Spirit get you back on the right path?

6. How can you receive correction from the Holy Spirit without resisting?

7. What attitudes could you change in order to receive God's grace in those times?

8. What is the best book on the subject of spiritual warfare and how often should we read it?

NOTES

Chapter 9

EVERYBODY IS SEARCHING FOR JESUS

EVERY FOLLOWER OF Christ has a story to tell of how they came to believe in and follow after Him. Here is my wife's story in her own words.

> As a child I grew up in a family that followed after Jesus. It was a great way to live and I have many wonderful memories of my childhood. Then as a young teen, I began to question the "rules" of this "straight and narrow" lifestyle. By age 17 or 18, I had turned my back on Jesus. I plunged headlong into the darkness of worldly experimentation and later, religious searching. I could not find peace, and my choices and searching only left me devastated. I kept thinking that if I only found that perfect relationship, or was in the right circumstances, or found that elusive belief system, I would be satisfied.
>
> Finally, broken and empty, I discovered again that Jesus, himself, loved me and had a plan for my life that was good and would make me whole and complete. After looking everywhere else, it was Jesus that I was looking for all the time.

1. Why is it that we think we will miss something if we follow Jesus?

2. Was it hard for you to believe that Jesus was what you were searching for?

3. Think about your "story".
   *Did you search for another way to "find your maker"?

   *What did it take to turn you around?

   *What difference was there in your life when you began to worship Jesus?

   *The enemy knows that humans desire Jesus, so what does he do to stop us?

   *What does he try on you?

Notes

Chapter 10

JUST HOW DIFFICULT IS THIS BATTLE?

I HAVE READ of many missionaries that have lost spouses, children, and even their own lives on the mission field. It is never easy to take such losses.

When a soldier signs up he needs to realize that he just signed his life away to the army. A Christian gives his life to the Captain of the Lord's Host in order to be in the Army of God. Our attitude should then be, "Whatever You want, Lord, that is what I want to do."

The great thing about this Captain is that He will cause you to want to do what He wants you to do.

I have a friend that wants to go to another country and work with struggling young people. She has been building toward that ministry for many years now and is looking for the next step. She is not even considering the difficulties that she may encounter; she just wants to go. She amazes me!

1. Knowing how big God is, how can we arise and work with Him to scatter His enemies?

2. Are there some areas of sacrifice that obedience to God's Word might require? Do you think that you could have joy in obedience in spite of the difficulties?

3. Timing is very important. Have you ever hesitated and missed the right timing, or have you ever jumped in too soon? How can we get better at God's timing?

4. Each part of the battle is difficult; which part seems to be most difficult to you?

5. Are you having fun yet? If not, can you think of what could change that?

6. In the text, there is one word that describes what it takes to have victory in obedience to God. That word is persistence. What does it take to have persistence until victory comes? Can you think of an example of persistence that brought victory in your life? If not, what was missing?

7. Jesus' disciples learned some things about who Jesus was when He calmed the storm. Can you see how this bigger picture of God's glory can help you overcome the difficulties that you may face?

NOTES

Chapter 11

THE MOST CRITICAL ISSUE

A GUY I know once said there is no spiritual warfare going on. What could I say to him? Later I thought that he must be blind to the war. It struck me that his spiritual discernment must be small. He sees all the garbage going on in the world, but only in the natural. Apparently he is completely oblivious to the spiritual realm. He needs to get in touch with the One who can give him spiritual discernment on the things of the Spirit. I believe he needs to know Jesus personally and not remotely.

When Jesus comes into your life He removes the veil. You become a spiritual person and the window of your soul gets a good cleaning so you can see clearly. There is nothing more important in a person's life for all eternity.

1. What would you say is the most critical issue of life?

2. Why don't we just go out there and help people?

3. How can we overcome our apathy? Our fear? Our hesitation? Our hindrances?

4. What is the supreme motive we can have in this life?

5. What is it that Jesus can do for people that we can't?

6. What can we do to reconcile people to Him?

7. Are there some specific people that God is reminding you about?

8. Are you willing for Him to give you His heart for them?

NOTES

Chapter 12

GREG'S PICTURE TO ME

WHEN DOES THE devil like to get you? When you're tired and sleepy? When you're cranky or busy? When you're distracted or angry? Or is it when you're set up for a trick? Yes! Yes! Yes! Yes! And Yes! How can we guard against this incessant onslaught? Be stalwart and stand firm in your faith. He is leaning on your door. He is crouching on your porch waiting for the next gotcha!

My son was right; I should have kept my eyes on the Lord. He is a much better warrior than I. I'm only a rank amateur in comparison.

1. What kind of trick did the enemy play on me?

2. Why did the devil provoke me into a fight?

3. What happened to me when I fought the enemy on my terms?

4. If the doctor couldn't help me but the church people could, what kind of problem was it?

5. Do you think Greg's vision was right?

6. Is it possible that the Lord changed a real problem into a temporary one?

7. Would God have dealt with the provocation of the enemy had I asked Him?

NOTES

WHICH WAY DID THE DEVIL GO?

Chapter 13

THE ENEMY LURKETH

SOME DREAMS ARE from too much pepperoni pizza. My grandmother once told me that she would dream of Indians circling the settlers, but that never happened to her. Dreams can come from the enemy. Dreams can come from the Lord. Some dreams have meaning. My dream had meaning; it showed me what the enemy was doing.

It is important to know the realm we are dealing with at any given time. We must learn to discern what is from the Lord, the devil, or another person. Handling the truth most of the time will give us a feel for what is true and what is not true. For instance, bank tellers are trained to discover counterfeit by handling real money.

If we remember a particular dream, we can ask the Lord for an interpretation. Keep your spiritual antenna up to find out what is happening. Warning: don't try to make every dream prophetic—they're not. Check out what you think before you tie it on to someone else. I know someone who said they had a dream that this person should marry that person. The marriage ended in total disaster. I didn't think it was a good idea, but they were convinced. Check it out. It might be too much pizza. It definitely was not from God.

1. Do you think the Lord can give you a dream to explain something?

2. What did I learn from my dream?

3. Who does the enemy seem to be concentrating on?

4. Does he know what kids want and how to provide it for them?

5. Does the devil use the truth on people? Or deceit?

6. Why do we need to tag a lie as a lie?

7. What kind of filter should we have on our mind?

8. Where does the enemy's power come from?

9. Who, then, can we turn to for strength against such a sneaky adversary?

NOTES

Chapter 14

THE UNSEEN BATTLE

STRANGE AS IT may seem, the battle is awesome, spiritual and unseen, but we can influence it. We have an inroad with the Lord. We can ask the Lord what He wants us to pray about, then pray according to what He says. We can ask what He wants us to do, then do what He asks. We can read our instructions in the Bible and follow them with the Lord's help.

It's an awesome battle, but we are not helpless. God has provided training and weapons so that we can become proficient warriors. At the same time the enemy has provided sufficient distraction to dilute that proficiency. He is counting on the fact that we too easily forget what we can't see. We must provoke ourselves to remain focused on the fight, and we will see victory.

1. What is this battle all about?

2. Since God is all powerful, why does he allow this battle to continue?

3. What schemes has the enemy used to distract you away from God in the past?

4. How did the Holy Spirit help you to see the truth and break away from those schemes?

5. Do you know if someone was praying for you at that time?

6. Is there someone that God wants you to be faithful to pray for now?

NOTES

ATTACKS AND COUNTERATTACKS

HAVE YOU SEEN children trying to get their way or to get one another in trouble by lying, blaming, pouting, acting snobbish, crying or manipulation? Well, these are similar to the tricks the enemy uses.

Somebody is trying to take "Under God" out of the Pledge of Allegiance. They are ready to take it to the Supreme Court with this and that reason. Tell me what is going on here?

We counterattack with prayer, finance and petitions. Our first counterattack needs to be prayer, then we find out the next step. We know who the strongest is, and He wants us to be involved in His victory.

1. If the devil tries to intimidate you and put you on the defensive, what is he really trying to do?

2. What is God's way of responding to this?

3. Are people our enemies? If not, how can we fight and be nice at the same time?

4. Who is our sure help in these perilous times?

5. What good is prayer in times of attack?

6. If we ask, will God get the victory?

NOTES

Chapter 16

SIN OF DIVISIVENESS

THERE IS A strong theme running through the Bible and every decent family. It is "unity." It is so important to get along that God invented a word: "love." 1 John 4:7-8 (NIV) tells us that God is love and he that does not love does not know God. That is how strongly God feels about getting along. He has tied himself to those who have this kind of unity.

Words can make or break unity, so we must be careful of what we say. Unity must be so deep in our hearts that divisive words can't even come out. Word choice should be honed to a science to be encouraging, loving, accepting, honoring and peaceful. Practice having a Christ-like attitude toward everybody and the right words will follow.

1. How much damage and pain can divisiveness bring?

2. If we are honest, there are always some "differences" and/or "issues" in our homes or local churches. How should we respond?

3. When we see disappointment and criticism move toward bitterness and gossip, how can we stop this process from continuing?

4. Is it possible to keep our thoughts positive when our emotions are involved? How can we change our supercharged emotions so that peace and love can prevail? Is there a way to help others do the same?

5. How can we increase in love and unity?

6. Keeping our mind on what is good and pure and lovely is one of the hardest things we can do. Have you succeeded in doing that in the middle of a difficult situation? How did you do it? If not, what can you do to change how you respond?

NOTES

Chapter 17

THE ALLEY TO STAN'S HOUSE

STAN'S RADIO WAS better than mine and he was allowed to listen to this show. My grandparents normally went to bed at 9 o'clock but they never worried where I was, so I felt free to stay until 10. Stan and I spent considerable time in the alley and knew every bush, fence and gate. I was not prepared to be there after dark, though, especially after listening to such a scary show.

I knew I was a fast runner and could outrun anything in the alley, except my imagination.

1. Fear produces more fear, but what should I have done?

2. What caused my imagination to run wild?

3. How could I have kept fear in check?

4. What in us tends to get out of control when the unknown strikes?

5. How deep can imaginations go if we don't rein them in?

6. What part do imaginations have in causing divisiveness?

7. 2 Cor. 10:5 (KJV) says, "Casting down imaginations, and every high thing that exalteth itself against the knowledge of God, and bringing into captivity every thought to the obedience of Christ." Is it possible that we may need to cast down some good imaginations too, so we can bring them into verification with truth?

8. Are you able to verify your imaginations with truth? Think and consider.

NOTES

HAS ANYBODY
SEEN MY SWORD?

Chapter 18

THE AUTHORITY AND POWER OF THE BELIEVER

PEOPLE ARE BUILT with a desire to have power and authority. Even a baby demands that its needs be met or exceeded. This is not bad, but there comes a time when these attitudes need to be disciplined and directed. To know power and authority people need to come under power and authority.

So it is in the Kingdom of God. The more we submit to authority, the more authority we get. The more we understand whose power and authority it really is, the more we can be involved with it. If we start taking credit for what God does, the only power and authority we have is whatever we can muster up in ourselves. Using our own power and authority is far less than what is available to us.

1. Do you believe that you can resist the devil?

2. Is it possible to muster up the power to resist the devil on your own?

3. When we receive the power and authority from God, what can we do with it?

4. How do you use this authority for defense? For offence?

5. Consider this statement in the chapter: "When you are in the prestigious position of being a servant of the Most High God, you can do anything He tells you to do. Most of it will have something to do with this battle for souls." Do you have something in mind that He may be telling you to do? Do you have confidence that He will help you do it?

NOTES

Chapter 19

SPIRITUAL WARFARE AND THE TRUTH

I LOVE THE truth. I set my mind to remember what I have heard. If I find out later that something is not true and have to erase it from my mind, I'm not a happy camper. I rarely read fiction because I don't want to confuse it with what I know to be real. I try to glean what could be truth from it and throw the rest away. Those mental gymnastics are laborious to me. My mind just doesn't work that way.

My habit is to read the Bible over and over to continually rinse my mind with the truth. It is easier to detect a lie that way. In my imagination I try to be careful that I don't get carried away with my own pet thoughts. I am able to stay in bounds by setting a limit that says untruth is sin.

1. How do we buckle on the truth?

2. Since the real battle begins in the believer's mind, why is truth such an important weapon?

3. How do we use it?

4. What is the number one law in spiritual warfare?

5. How does choice play a role?

6. When truth is the filter in our minds, what happens to stuff that is in there?

7. Are there areas in your life where the weapon of truth needs to be applied?

8. Explain how truth is a defensive weapon. An offensive weapon.

<u>NOTES</u>

Chapter 20

SPIRITUAL WARFARE AND RIGHTEOUSNESS

ONE OF MY favorite books is Romans; it is very descriptive of righteousness. Romans 6:16, 19, 22 gives the progression from obedience to righteousness to holiness to eternal life. You start with obedience in a particular area until you are consistent. Then you move forward in righteousness to holiness to eternal life. We work on them all and progress separately in each department. Eternal life is our final reward.

Here's one way I describe righteousness: "doing what is right when nobody is looking."

God helps us when we confess our sin. He forgives our sin, then turns right around and cleans us from unrighteousness. You can't beat a deal like that. The enemy has a hard time when we are righteous. What can he accuse us of? You are in a win-win situation.

1. What is the first step to receiving righteousness?

2. How does righteousness fit between obedience and holiness?

3. Why is righteousness important for defense in spiritual warfare?

4. How can unrighteousness "deliver a crushing blow" to an otherwise productive and effective thrust into the enemy's camp?

5. What will God do for us when we are righteous in trials?

6. What happens to us when we become self-righteous?

7. Is there anything in your life that you need to adjust to continue to progress in righteousness? Think and consider.

NOTES

SPIRITUAL WARFARE AND THE GOSPEL OF PEACE

WHAT A WEAPON! You just stiff-arm the devil when you have peace.

The Gospel is so powerful that it can yank people right over the wall of the devil's kingdom. The enemy is powerless against the Gospel. He was beat by it 2000 years ago, and he is still taking a whooping from it.

I read that in 2007 alone, more than 50 million people came to Christ. What a blow to the enemy's ego, who is trying to make you think that he is winning. The devil is beaten by the Gospel. But we will have to keep up the pressure, because people are being born every day that haven't heard the Gospel of Peace. This is the good news of the Prince of Peace, Jesus.

1. Why is peace so hard for the enemy to penetrate?

2. What is the Gospel of Peace?

3. Why is the enemy so fired up against the Gospel?

4. How do we put on this Gospel of Peace?

5. Do you think that the enemy is going to let you get away with using the Gospel as a weapon to shrink his kingdom? What will he do, and how will you combat it?

6. Are you going to win or lose if you use the Gospel against the devil?

7. Have you learned a simple Gospel presentation yet?

NOTES

SPIRITUAL WARFARE USING THE SHIELD OF FAITH

THE PREACHER SAYS, "Build your faith." That's easy to say, but how do you do it? The Bible tells us that by hearing the Word we build our faith. When we really "hear" something, we do it. We can't just walk away saying, "Oh that was a nice word," and then not obey it. "Faith" is like "believe" in that there is an action required in response to the word.

1. What weapon can we use to fend off these "fiery darts"?

2. If faith is the key to this area of defense, think about scriptures and scriptural principles that you know that will combat these attacks. How can rehearsing them build your faith?

3. We can use the Word of God to combat the enemy. It builds our faith and gives us power to strike down enemy strongholds. Can you see how that can make our Shield of Faith an offensive weapon as well?

4. Think about the different forms of the Word of God. Are you able to build your faith with each of these? If not, what hinders you? Do you believe God will help you in that?

5. The conclusion to the chapter reads, "So it all boils down to this: God offers the shield of faith to all who will believe, as a weapon to defend against the enemy and as a weapon to destroy his stronghold." Can you see an area in your life where you can apply the shield of faith right now? In the future?

NOTES

Chapter 23

SPIRITUAL WARFARE WITH THE HELMET OF SALVATION

THE BIBLE HAS a lot to say about the mind. Renew your mind; have the mind of Christ; pray with our mind; sing with our mind and God's mind. We can see that the Lord is concerned about our mind. It's the control tower for the rest of our being. The mind is the garage for our conscience. The mind is the origin for our thoughts, words and actions. That's why it is so important to protect.

As the helmet protects our minds, so must we protect our helmet. The care and feeding of our helmet is to polish and adjust it daily by the Word, prayer and obedience. We must appropriate it daily. Our salvation is not a one time happening, but moment by moment we are saved. Treat that helmet with utmost respect. And for Heaven's sake, don't take it off.

1. How do we get a helmet?

2. What protection does the helmet provide for the Christian who puts it on and keeps it on?

3. What happens when the helmet is taken off?

4. Explain how the helmet is both a defensive and an offensive weapon.

5. In the context of this chapter, why does the new Christian need to be encouraged and trained?

6. When we come to God for help, what is His response?

7. Where does this joy come from?

8. How does reading the "battle manual" (The Bible) strengthen the helmet?

9. What part of us does the helmet protect?

NOTES

Chapter 24

THE BIBLE IS MORE THAN A SWORD

I LOVE THE Bible. It has been a constant companion and friend for 42 years, and every year my respect for God and His Word has only increased. Without a photographic memory, I need to read it through about once a year. That's the only way I can keep the principles of the Bible current in my brain. One time as I was reading through the Bible, I looked for scriptures about God as Father. I spent every moment I possibly could for about 2 ½ months searching for these scriptures, resulting in a new relationship with God as Father.

Reading the Bible makes my life more stable as I gain truth and understanding of how God feels about me and how I should feel about others.

1. Is the Bible just a book full of pages with words on them?

2. How is the Bible a defensive weapon?

3. How is the Bible an offensive weapon?

4. How can we benefit from the Word of God that is "sharper than a two-edged sword"?

5. When we use the Bible as a sword, what cautions should we remember?

6. It's important to learn God's attitudes. Do you have attitudes that need to be changed? Ways that need adjusting? Think and consider.

Notes

Chapter 25

SPIRITUAL WARFARE AND PRAYER

NOT LONG INTO my prayer journey, I discovered that prayer was never meant to be a monolog. I needed some answers. I ran out of things to pray about. I didn't know how to pray. Many problems came up that I couldn't solve, and that was good. I positioned myself and said, "I'm done talking; now you talk." Soon I realized that the Holy Spirit had more important things to say than I did. As a result, listening became a much larger part of my prayer than before.

Encouragement and direction is what I need to guide me through my daily life. Answers and warnings are immediately available with this two way corridor operating. Spiritual warfare needs a quick understanding of what's happening, so opening up the other half of prayer is essential.

1. How is prayer a weapon?

2. If we don't always know what to do, where should we go for the answers?

3. Would you say your prayer life is mostly a monolog? If so, is it possible to change it to a dialog with God?

4. John 10:3b-4 (NIV) says, "He calls his own sheep by name and leads them out. When he has brought out all his own, he goes on ahead of them, and his sheep follow him because they know his voice." How can we learn to hear and recognize Jesus voice?

5. If Jesus is your commander in this war, how important is your communication with Him?

6. Did this chapter challenge you in your prayer life? What steps can you take to implement these changes?

NOTES

Chapter 26

THE WEAPONS OF PRAISE

PRAISING THE LORD is right and necessary. In our lives, if praise isn't happening, things are out of order. After all, when we praise we express our trust in the One who is able to save, deliver and help us in every situation.

When God is operating in our life, what can come up against us and prevail? Nobody and nothing can overpower God. When we consciously call out to God in praise, He is right there. He sees the problem. He acts on the problem. He knows what we want to happen, but He wants us to voice it. That way it is cooperation. When we voice our need and our trust in Him, it changes our focus and our attitudes. The problem gets much smaller when we are rehearsing His great faithfulness and love for us. When we look for Him and express our trust in Him, our eyes can see his salvation, however He chooses to move upon our circumstances. That strengthens our relationship with Him and increases our trust (faith) even more. Praise Him early in the situation.

1. What does "Hallelujah" mean?

2. Why is praise to the Lord so powerful?

3. Explain why the verbal expression of praise to the Lord is so effective in our lives.

4. What happens when we say negative things? What about positive things?

5. When things go wrong, what should our first response be? Why do you think we forget to do it?

6. Praise to the Lord gets what in harmony with what?

NOTES

Chapter 27

DON'T COUNT THE ANGELS OUT

I HAVE HEARD car stories about the intervention of angels. For instance, two friends of mine started to cross an intersection and stopped. A car was coming directly toward them. The car went around them at square angles heading the same way and at the same speed. What about the car coming toward them for a head on crash? It went over them.

One time, I stopped at a four-way stop and hesitated a couple seconds. A car came barreling through the intersection about 80 miles an hour from the left. I hesitated another couple seconds and another car did the same thing. I looked again, thanked the Lord, and drove through the intersection. Angels are on the job.

1. What are angels?

2. What is their job?

3. Can they help you in the war?

4. How did they help Dave?

5. What did they do for Burdell?

6. Will angels help a person who is not saved yet?

7. Do we serve angels? Or do we serve God, and the angels serve us?

NOTES

WE NEED A PLAN

Chapter 28

NO STRATEGY IS NOT GOOD STRATEGY

"ASSUMING" CAN QUICKLY get us into trouble. It's good to expect the Lord to lead us, but if we are going in the wrong direction, where is He going to lead us? We must first of all find out what the Lord wants us to do and where to go. Then we need to make some preparation for the assignment.

I knew a missionary who prepared a full system of Sunday school material. The Lord sent him to Indonesia, where he set up many Sunday schools in the area. The project was successful because he prepared. He later went to Fiji and did the same. God made a difference because the missionary was prepared.

1. If we have no strategy, what kind of strategy do we have?

2. Where do we find out what the strategy for this battle is?

3. Can we have only one strategy for everything we do and everywhere we go? Why? Or why not?

4. What determines what our strategy should look like?

5. How do we get specific strategy?

6. In the book, I mention some important aspects of battle strategy. What are they?

7. If we see one method doesn't work anymore, what should we do?

NOTES

Chapter 29

THE BATTLE PLAN

DURING WORLD WAR II the allied generals made Germany think they were going to attack from the north. Then they made a full assault straight into France and caught the enemy off guard. A similar thing happened in the Gulf War. The general put troops in the gulf for a frontal attack on Kuwait. At the same time, he secretly put troops in the desert for a rear attack. By the time Iraq realized the trap, it was too late, and they lost the offensive in 100 hours. King David did the same thing to the Philistines.

The battle plan has to be well planned out, with the Lord as our Master Planner.

1. What is the real purpose of the battle?

2. Can we do this on our own?

3. In the book, I listed four things we need to know to win this battle. What are they?

4. How can we detect the enemy's schemes in our lives?

5. Who can we trust to lead us in the midst of the battle?

6. What happens to us if we don't know the power of God?

7. How can we receive help when we are wounded?

8. Where is the direct communication line in this battle?

9. What is the best way to limit the enemy's ability to harm us?

NOTES

Chapter 30

WHAT'S YOUR PART IN ALL OF THIS?

PEOPLE SEEM TO think they are insignificant and weak, so they don't pursue God's purpose for them in the Heavenly scheme of the battle. Don't forget, we may be only one person in the Lord's army, but we are a real and necessary part. We have abilities and have been trained to do a job. God is counting on us to help. He, being Creator God, can train up someone else, but that is not His original plan.

What we need to know is that God is not second best in this battle—He is first. This battle is a testing ground for people. Who is going to come up to the challenge? Who is going to grit it through? Who is going to shrink back? We need to grab ourselves by the nape of the neck and say, "We are on the winning side, and we are going to win." Find your part and do it with courage and valor.

1. What has God given you that you can use in the battle?

2. How do we give God glory with what He has given us?

3. When you do your part and you see good things happen, what does that build in you?

4. On your way to your highest calling, what do you do?

5. What happens when you do the best you can with what you've got?

6. What has God called you to do in your church? In the world? Think and consider.

NOTES

Chapter 31

THE ARMY MUST BE DISCIPLINED

THE PASTOR'S RESPONSIBILITY is direct; he is the one who is supposed to be preparing his flock to do the work of the ministry. If not, then he does everything alone, while the congregation and the Kingdom suffer. When we go to church, we need to know that the lessons we are learning train us to minister.

Jesus chose twelve disciples to train. These twelve turned the world upright for the Gospel. These disciplined men went out and did what they saw the Master do, and the known world was changed. It is the same today.

1. Why do we need extensive training and discipline?

2. Is it really the soldier's choice which branch of the army to be in or which job to do?

3. The world says you can do what you want. Is that true in the army of God?

4. Who should we ultimately trust to train us, even if we see a man in front of us?

5. How can we keep an "I don't care" attitude from setting in?

6. How well should we know our training manual, the Bible?

7. Is our training ever really over?

NOTES

Chapter 32

DISCIPLINE TO BE AWARE

WHEN WE ARE spiritually alive we can detect spiritual things. We can detect when the Holy Spirit talks or when there is an evil spirit lurking close by. In this spiritual war we must be sensitive to both realms. When we detect an evil spirit we don't turn and fight it, but give it immediately to the Lord. With praise and petition we speak to the Lord, then He fights the battle.

I heard about an evangelist who said he stopped rebuking the devil every service because the demons all came for the show. When he just praised the Lord and filled the atmosphere with worship, the demons were rendered powerless. They certainly didn't like that.

1. How easy is it to be open to spiritual attack?

2. Have you gotten tired of putting on the spiritual armor everyday?

3. How can we be aware of the possibility of an attack?

4. How can we train our mind to be sensitive to any cracks in our defense?

5. Some counterfeits are very genuine looking. How can we tell the difference?

6. We need to reinforce "right" standards daily. How can we do that?

7. What happens to people who bathe themselves in complacency?

NOTES

Chapter 33

BOOT CAMP

NOBODY LIKES BOOT camp. It is hard, and you have to do things you don't like to do, but it is good to learn to follow orders. You will probably have to do things that have little or nothing to do with your ministry. Attitudes and patience are some of man's main problems. Boot camp, (however that works out in your life) is a time of searching and stretching, which is necessary to know spiritual direction and distance. Embrace this time in your life as most valuable and as something that can't be achieved any other way.

1. Why should we "stream to God's boot camp"?

2. When we come to the point that we know we need to be trained, what do we do?

3. What are some of the indications that the training that you are getting is good, powerful and lasting?

4. Is the trainer modeling what he tells you to do?

5. What areas of you are being trained and changed?

6. Boot camp can't cover everything, so who should we depend upon to further and complete the training?

7. Where and how do we get fed by the Word of God?

NOTES

Chapter 34

GOOD TACTICS ARE ESSENTIAL

WHEN WE COUNTER the tactics of the enemy with the Lord's actions, we win. Hezekiah and Jehoshaphat both took their battle to the Lord and they won. Daniel prayed, worshipped, and confessed the sins of Israel, and the angels fought the battle in the heavenlies. We don't counter the devil's tactics with our own strength, because that is the fight he wants. He is coaxing us into a fight that he can't lose and we can't win.

Our fight against the devil should be resisting him and calling on the Lord.

1. Why do you need good tactics in this spiritual war?

2. What is one of the first tactics each side tries to use?

3. What are the next tactics that the enemy uses?

4. The Kingdom of God has similar tactics. How are they different?

5. How do the Lord's tactics counter the enemy's?

6. One thing the enemy does is push on you until you weaken. How does the Lord counter this attack?

7. How do we counter the lies of the enemy?

8. Will daily Bible study and prayer help the Christian stay strong? How?

9. If we continually resist the enemy, what will he have to do? With the Lord's help, can we do this?

NOTES

Chapter 35

WE NEED MARCHING ORDERS

ONE THING FOR sure is that we don't pick our fights. I did this once when I was a kid. This guy ran into my bike and I jumped off and said, "Put up your dukes." He did and I got beat so quickly that I didn't even realize what hit me. So I can imagine that the devil is similar. If we started a fight with him on his terms we would be quickly beaten.

When we sense a battle brewing, we need to immediately turn to the Lord. The battle can even be fun when we are participating with the Lord and watching Him get the victory.

The Lord wants us to be with Him in the fight as if He were saying, "Watch this move. How do you like this punch? See, the enemy can't handle this one. Watch them drop. Here comes another one over to our side." Our involvement is little more than being a spectator, when we let the "powerful expert" handle it.

1. What two things do we need to ask the Lord when problems come?

2. How important is it to always check with the Captain of the Lord's Host before getting involved in this part of the battle?

3. How difficult a time do we have when we compromise the orders we know to follow?

4. Do we get the victory if we don't fight?

5. If you obey the Captain, what can you expect?

6. How do we know if we are supposed to fight the battle from near or far?

7. What are you best suited for, and where do you think you should go?

NOTES

Chapter 36

THE MOVEMENT OF THE TROOPS

IT IS SOMETIMES difficult for Christians to know when and where to move. My wife and I made a move recently that didn't make sense in the natural. It was to another county, further away from our work, our church, our close friends, and our grandchildren. Friends asked the obvious question, "Why?" I had reasons and excuses which they graciously accepted.

We knew in our heart we were supposed to move and the Lord is slowly revealing why. Many times obedience precedes explanation.

1. The troop movement should always be covered by prayer. Do you have a specific assignment to cover?

2. When God's troops move against the enemy, what is the enemy going to do in return?

3. If you have a weakness in your defense what could happen?

4. Should you go on a mission or ministry if the Lord doesn't go?

5. The enemy hates it when Christians go on mission trips, so what is he going to try to do?

6. How many "missions" need to be covered by prayer? How much prayer?

7. What other ways might you be able to help?

8. What are some steps you need to take when going on a mission?

9. Don't help the enemy think up ways to mess up missions, ministries, or people back home. What must we be careful of?

10. When someone goes on a mission, have them pass around flyers for each supporting person to sign saying that they will pray for the team sent out. Then hand the flyers back to the missionaries for further prayer. A signed contract is not easily forgotten.

NOTES

Chapter 37

FOLLOW THE LEADER

WHEN WE MOVED into the next county we became part of another team. Our new pastor has a different style of preaching, but the message is just as good. We have a little different purpose in this new place.

After moving, I understood that Jesus was saying, "I want you to go over here and be part of my Kingdom." Jesus is the owner of His church and can put His people wherever He wants them. It doesn't have to make sense to us. The Lord Jesus put the pastor in place and positioned us under him. We, then, are part of each other's ministry. We are there to be trained to do the work of the ministry to fulfill our corner of the Kingdom of God.

1. Why does God's army need to be organized?

2. Why do we need to be submitted to our leaders?

3. When Christians advance in unity the devil loses. But what can happen during the advance?

4. What does the devil try to stir up? How can we stop his tricks?

5. In offences, we still must have a good attitude. How can we do that?

6. What are we supposed to do for our leaders?

7. What are our spiritual leaders supposed to do for us?

NOTES

Chapter 38

TO ADVANCE THE KINGDOM

TO BE IN Christ is the safest place in the world. In that safe place it is important to walk and work in harmony with one another. We really need each other. Love is the strongest bond we can have. That love will accomplish great things for the Kingdom.

With Christ and our relationship with Him a priority in our life we can do whatever He asks. Obedience to our Captain will help our side win much faster. The Bible says to hasten the coming of the Lord.

1. How can we hinder the enemy's aggression against us?

2. What are the tools the enemy uses on the believer to try to cause him to be ineffective?

3. No matter who we are or where we are, our object is to advance the Kingdom of God. What does that involve?

4. How simple is it to lead a person one step closer to salvation?

5. Peter did pretty well at his first time walking on water. How did you do the first time you attempted to "Come" when Jesus called you to do something out of your comfort zone?

6. Did you learn to seek the Lord's help first before you tried it the next time?

7. The text says, "Jesus may not ask you to walk on water, but what He does ask will take the same kind of faith and dependence on Him." How can we make our response be the most effective?

8. Will you have enough tools to do the job Jesus calls you to do? Are there some steps that you can take to help you be better prepared to respond?

9. Is the support of your local church helpful when you are on a mission? How?

<u>NOTES</u>

Chapter 39

NEVER LET YOUR GUARD DOWN

I ATTENDED SERVICE at a particular church one Sunday and noticed that five people had broken bones. I said to myself, *It looks as if nobody is praying for these people; I have a job to do.* I prayed for everybody in the church every day. Later, at our new church, I saw three ladies slip and fall one Sunday morning. Déjà vu all over again. I started praying for each member of that congregation every day as well. There were fewer accidents in both groups, plus I was able to remember their names better than ever before.

Don't look now, but you are being watched. There is somebody out there that wants to trip you up. Cover your pastor, the congregation, and anyone else who comes to mind with prayer. The enemy is not sovereign but he is sneaky.

It's good to be pro-active in prayer. Pray what you think you should about something that hasn't happened yet. Pray for the outcome before it's finished. Pray against what you don't want to happen. Pray what you hear the Holy Spirit saying. If the Holy Spirit reveals to you a judgment coming, He may want you to pray for the situation to change so He won't have to judge. Pray creatively into situations you want to see changed.

1. When a person goes into battle, is it time to relax? How about right after winning a big victory?

2. Why is the spiritual leader more vulnerable than the followers?

3. We know that God is greater than the devil, but does this mean the enemy is a pushover?

4. If God tells me to go, is He going with me? Does He go with me when I go on my own or in my own timing?

5. We need to be open and aware of the voice of the Lord at all times. Are there times when you are not listening? How can you learn to hear and respond quickly?

6. A saying in the world is "the bigger they are, the harder they fall." Is this true in God's kingdom?

7. Who will the enemy pick on if he can't get the leader? Pray for whomever the Holy Spirit puts on your mind. It might save that person's life.

NOTES

Chapter 40

IN CASE OF SETBACKS

MISTAKES? OH YES! The other night driving on a two lane road, I pulled over to let a car pass. The side of the road was wet and my ABS brakes jerked trying to stop in the wet grass. My wife exclaimed, "Bill! (the emphasis is mine.) What are you doing?"

"Well, he was going faster than me so I let him pass." I got back on the road and acted as if nothing happened. To me there was no emergency, but it was quite unexpected to her. Maybe the normal reaction would have been to cuss the guy out for dogging my car, but everything was OK. I don't cuss anyway. I know God is in control.

How does the Father react when we goof? He forgives us. I learned a good lessen a long time ago. I learned to forgive myself. God doesn't condemn me, so it's a sin to condemn myself.

1. As Christians, when we make mistakes do we give up, or find out what went wrong and fix it?

2. When you have problems and the Lord comes to your rescue, what gets built up?

3. When there is a setback, what do the champions do? What do you do? What should you do? Can you think of something you can change in order to respond like a champion?

4. Setbacks are negative in nature, but how else can you gain that experience? Think about how valuable your setbacks have been in your life? Were you able to "use" them correctly?

5. How will God pull them out and turn them for good?

6. What grows in God's forgiveness?

7. Who is bigger than your setbacks?

NOTES

Chapter 41

WE ARE NOT IGNORANT

WHEN WE KNOW who we really are, we are more resilient to attacks. When the enemy defames your character you can know it's a lie. Only the Lord can show you who you really are. You can learn your strong points and weak points and not be unhappy that you are not a movie star or a rocket scientist. The Lord wants to train you to be the best "you" that you can be.

We live in a world full of pride and degradation, so we need to brace ourselves in the love of the Lord and let the offences roll off us like water off a duck's back. This is easy to say, but hard to do. That's why we need help from above to be less and less ignorant.

1. Does the Bible mean that we don't need to be ignorant of the devil's schemes?

2. When the devil says to people, "You are mine and you can't change that," is that a lie? Does it have to stay that way?

3. What kind of a father is the devil? How about God (the Almighty Creator)?

4. Why does the devil trick you into thinking you are somebody else?

5. Why does he prompt you into comparisons and discouragements?

6. Why does he want us to think that people are worthless? How is this being played out in our society?

7. Why does he prompt us to sin in our relationships?

8. How can we learn to depend upon God's wisdom and not be ignorant of the devil's wiles?

NOTES

Chapter 42

GREATER IS HE THAT IS IN US

HOW EASY IT is for us to forget that there are angels watching over us. It's hard to remember what we can't see. The Great Almighty Creator God, his Son Jesus and Holy Spirit are inside Christians. Why would we ever be fearful with all that power so near? Faith is the life blood between the Lord, our conscience, and our soul, spirit and mind. Faith needs to be a vibrant and fresh fluid surging through our spiritual veins. Faith must be renewed often through our relationship with the Lord and the power of the Holy Spirit.

1. How much can God protect His people?

2. Who is strongest in the conflict?

3. What attracts demons to your area?

4. Is the real problem what we see or what we don't see? Is it the manifestation or the root?

5. In our town and in our body there are underlying things that must be dealt with and resolved before what we see will be good. How can we do this?

6. What's the most effective, long-term answer to having a bigger army with more soldiers?

7. What can happen if we allow sin to remain and not deal with it?

8. Who is the only solution for fixing our soul and spirit?

NOTES

Chapter 43

THE UPWARD CLIMB IS THE EASIEST

LIFE IS HARD. Being a Christian or a non-Christian is hard. The choice is which hardness do you want to choose? We discipline our body to endure life. We discipline our soul for either good or evil. We can discipline our spirit to live for Christ. So do we want to live a partially disciplined or a completely disciplined life? The choice is ours. Just remember, the more Godly discipline we endure the better we become in all areas.

Personally I like the easiest way. To work hard and make a good living is not difficult for me. I did find life was very hard for me without the Lord and going to church. I met the Lord when I was very young, but flopped around in the world for a while. That was tough. It was not too long before I realized it was easier to live life with the Lord's help. I found out from that experience that the upward climb toward Jesus was all in all the easiest life.

1. What makes going along with the crowd seem easier?

2. What kind of standards do people want to force on you?

3. Why is it harder to resist flowing with the tide of popular opinion?

4. Do "always wanting more" and lusting after the latest things satisfy the need, want, or pride in us, or should we choose to resist the tendency?

5. What does "trusting in the Lord" imply?

6. Trusting in the Lord takes away anxiety and brings peace, so is that easier?

NOTES

Chapter 44

THE SPIRITUAL PART OF THIS SPIRITUAL WAR

A PERSON CAN tune their spirit into something good or bad. The Christian keeps his or her spirit tuned into the Lord. A person can also tune their spirit into other spirits, so it is important to keep discerning what is good and what is not. The Christian needs to train him or herself to hear the Holy Spirit by salvation, learning about the Lord, getting to know the Lord, praying, and hearing the Word.

The other part of the spiritual war is to obey what you hear the Holy Spirit saying. Many times this takes more faith and fortitude in the spirit than in the natural. When God wants us to do something it is many times too hard for our flesh to perform. So we go back to God and ask for help. This is what He really wanted all along. He wants us to come to Him and work with Him.

1. Have you ever noticed something that you couldn't see but you sensed?

2. Would you say this spiritual sensation is a ghost in the house or a person's attitude?

3. This happens in the heavenlies as well, so then who is the responsible party here, people or spirits?

4. Do we battle the positive attitudes or the negative attitudes? Which are the most destructive?

5. Should we do battle in the flesh or the spirit?

6. Can we use our word to do battle in the spiritual? Explain.

7. What kind of words open up a crack for the enemy to use against us?

8. What should we do with garbage words?

9. How do we stay on top of this spiritual war?

NOTES

Chapter 45

THE ULTIMATE PURPOSE

THROUGH THE WISDOM of God we were created. Humans were created with just enough body, soul, and spirit to operate on earth and communicate with God. But God wants more than that. He wants us to be with Him forever. By design, this is way beyond our given ability. So to those who have chosen to come to Him, His way, He has given us access. We need to ask and follow instructions.

1. What does God use for redemption?

2. How long has this been in the plan?

3. Who are the vehicles that God uses to implement this plan?

4. What is the alternative to receiving the Gospel?

5. Is taking the Gospel around the world an easy task?

6. What is the benefit for those who receive the Gospel?

7. What do we do if we are rejected?

8. What must we receive from God to continue taking the Gospel?

9. What has God placed in all people to help them receive the Gospel?

NOTES

Chapter 46

OBEDIENCE EQUALS VICTORY

I'M REMINDED THAT in WWI they started using balloons and airplanes to find out what the enemy was doing. That way they could see over the hills. Many times we don't know what we should do. We need the Lord to show us the way. If we find out what His way is and do it as instructed, we are assured a victory. If we try to do it on our own ability, it's a 50-50 chance. That is equal to, "Good luck." We desire better than that. We want 100 percent of what we do to be right and beneficial.

1. Was Joshua given orders that resulted in victory? Did they make sense?

2. Was this going to be a natural or a spiritual victory?

3. Was there any indication as to the outcome of the battle?

4. What was the key to Joshua's victory?

5. What are the steps to victories in our lives?

6. Must we maintain a willingness to obey in order to hear and do the will of God?

7. Do we have to see the whole picture in order to obey?

8. Can we usually fight these battles on our own?

9. Who is hurt when we disobey?

10. What should you do when you see disobedience raise its ugly head? What will happen if it continues?

NOTES

Chapter 47

ARMY DIET

EVERY DAY WE need to challenge ourselves in body, soul and spirit. We challenge our body with proper exercise and food. We challenge our soul in how we act and think. We challenge our spirit in learning about God and communicating with Him. If we become lax in any of these areas then atrophy begins to set in. With lack of use there comes weakness in that area.

In spiritual warfare it is important to keep up our spiritual nourishment.

1. How important is a good diet to a regular army?

2. What kind of diet does a spiritual army need to have?

3. How can we know what is the truth, so we aren't fooled by lies?

4. How does a spiritual soldier get a balanced diet?

5. Since the spiritual soldier needs to obey, who helps him do that?

6. If Jesus said that His food was to do the Father's will; should we do any less? Will He help us with that?

NOTES

THE PLOT THICKENS

Chapter 48

IS THE CONFLICT JUST IN YOUR MIND?

THIS BATTLE IS real, with real hostages. Whole countries are involved in the fray. In some countries it's more obvious than in others. Each country's battle comes in different forms—some physical, some mental, and some spiritual. In countries where one group tries to kill another, it is in plain view. Where there is education and affluence, money and the things of life take the place of God in the lives of people. In other countries, the people worship idols or millions of Gods, and are locked into poverty and hopelessness.

The conflicts in every country start in the mind, in the way the people view the world. They start there, but quickly are lived out in the physical realm.

1. Do we sometimes wonder where the battle is?

2. Is it a mind thing or from something higher?

3. Who is most likely to be attacked spiritually?

4. Shouldn't we be more aggressive in battling the enemy for the sake of the young?

5. What becomes an open door for the enemy?

6. Where do we need to go when we see where the devil is at work?

7. Does the enemy ever give up?

8. In spite of the hardness of battle, how do we know that we will win?

9. Is this conflict an accident?

10. Why is God allowing it?

NOTES

Chapter 49

A CHALLENGE TO THE COMPLACENT

HOW DO YOU feel? Do you feel like your life is going down the tube? Do you feel like you are in the process and on the verge of doing great things for Christ? Or are you somewhere in between? It is important for you to stir up some energy to get going. Getting off of top dead center is going to take some pushing to get out of your comfort zone.

We need to be listening in the spirit for the commendation, "Well done thou good and faithful servant." You can hear it if you keep your spirit open to the Holy Spirit. You keep your spirit open by talking and listening.

Flash! The Holy Spirit will direct you to do something that you want to do, because He causes you to want to do it. You can forecast fulfillment in it. You will be led forth in peace. It's going to be good.

1. Do you know what you are supposed to be doing in the Kingdom of God?

2. Where do we start to find out what our job is?

3. What good does seeking God do, in finding His will for our lives?

4. How does obedience open the channel to God's desire for you?

5. How do we plug up that channel?

6. Will pleasing God bring you more pleasure than you could have on your own?

7. When you think you are worthless and good for nothing, what happens to you?

8. Is that the truth or a lie from the enemy that you have believed?

9. Can a person level out in the Kingdom of God? Why? Why not?

10. Where will you end up if you don't progress in the Kingdom?

NOTES

Chapter 50

DEDICATION TO THE BATTLE

DID YOU EVER take the "Discover Your God-Given Gifts" test? This is a great book by Don and Katie Fortune. There are several books, but this is the one I like for finding out what you can do the best and how the others relate. This is important if you want to be the most effective in the Kingdom of God.

Knowing what you like to do and what you are good at will give you peace and direction in your quest for your niche in the Kingdom. Dedication will then come easily.

1. Who makes the choice to fight or faint in the battle?

2. What do we hear if we listen to the flesh?

3. Everybody has abilities. What are yours?

4. Can you dedicate your abilities to the battle for souls?

5. Who can we ask to find out what we are supposed to do?

6. Will we always understand why He directs us this way or that?

7. Can we ever really know the whole picture?

8. Must we then take our orders on faith?

9. How do we cultivate our testimony?

10. Should we hone our skills, our soul and our spirit, to be as dedicated to the Lord as possible?

NOTES

Chapter 51

THE WONDERFUL WORLD OF THE MIND

THE BRAIN IS the control center for the body. What our body wants to do has to be directed by our mind. Where the mind goes, the body will follow. It is very important that our mind, will, and emotions are all working together in agreement with our spirit. If not, there will be conflict and confusion within us; we will be open to the enemy's attacks, and we will be shut down in the battle.

1. Where does any action first get developed?

2. Even when we have "winning knowledge," what is necessary to actually win?

3. What can we do to keep our mind from taking us in the wrong direction?

4. Should we make Jesus Lord of our mind first and foremost?

5. If we don't make Jesus Lord of our mind, then who is?

6. How do we clear our conscience?

7. How do we keep our mind clean?

8. What do we do with imaginations that are unruly?

NOTES

Chapter 52

"WHERE'S THE POWER?" SCREAMED THE PREACHER

I CAN'T REMEMBER what his point was, but this is a cry of humanity from ages past. After a while we realize there is more to it than just yelling for it. Some work harder for more power than others do. You know, what we are really looking for is something we can't muster up anyway.

A long term relationship with the Lord begins to give us a clue. All power belongs to God. If we want in on it, we must do it His way. There is power to heal—when He says so. There is power in the Holy Spirit in His time and His way. We may find out about it. We may ask for it. We may see it. We may be involved in it. But only the Holy Spirit has the power.

The preacher was not wrong to ask where the power was, but he had the answer in his hand. The Bible tells about it.

1. How long has this quest for more power been going on? Wasn't that the cause behind the devil being thrown out of heaven?

2. What is the very starting point and basis for being on God's side and learning His ways?

3. How can we appropriate the power of God?

4. What is a big key to walking in God's power? Can you think of times when you "tested your footing in obedience?"

5. What are the ways we learn God's will?

6. What will obedience to the Word of God do for your relationship with Him?

7. What should be our first priorities if we want to gain more of the presence of God?

8. Can you know what He wants to do and let His power flow through you to do it? Can you hear what He is saying and let His power flow through you to say it?

9. Consider this: Is there something you already know He wants to do or say through you? Are you willing to do it? Go ahead and do it, and know that He will help you.

<u>NOTES</u>

Chapter 53

EVERYTHING FOR THE BATTLE

IN THE AREA of money, it's very important to do what the Lord puts on our heart. There are a number of principles at work here:

- God gives seed to the sower.
- Bring the tithes into the storehouse and see how God opens up the gates of heaven for you.
- 10 percent to the priest, 10 percent to the House of the Lord, 10 percent every three years for the poor.
- The people of Corinth gave to help Paul on his mission trips.
- The Macedonia churches gave generously to help the poor in spite of their own poverty.
- And many more.

Always seek to know where and when God calls you to give. If all will be diligent to do this, there will be more than enough.

There are many different ways to serve: time, talent, strength, organization, abilities, and more. We can serve people in the church or out of the church. Sometimes it is a sacrifice, but we must ask ourselves, "Is that so much to ask?"

1. How can we have a soldier's mentality?

2. Doesn't it make sense to be careful of our resources? Can you think of some area of your life where you could conserve your resources by doing with less, and then spend those resources on the battle?

3. How do we become better soldiers in the Kingdom?

4. How can we have fun in the Kingdom of God while working in the world? Think about the lives you have touched. Doesn't it bring you joy?

5. I think the challenges are terrific in the Kingdom and the battle, so as you have been learning and exercising your soul and spirit, can you feel yourself "getting buff?"

6. The more we learn to move in the Spirit, the more we need six things. What are these six things?

7. Jesus made the ultimate sacrifice for the Kingdom, so what did He gain?

NOTES

THIS IS HEAVEN

Chapter 54

BATTLE TO ITS CONCLUSION

THINGS WILL CONCLUDE. Time and life will conclude. The spiritual war will be concluded. You gotta know God will win. There is purpose for this battle, so don't lose heart. Myself, I tend to find out how to enjoy hard things. I think it helps me through them. I have some engineer genes in me that enjoy figuring out how to do difficult things. My mom tells me that my grandfather would spend ten minutes trying to figure out how to do a five minute job in five minutes or less. I think he could do anything mechanical.

The Bible tells us who the winner is, so we don't have to worry. We can have peace knowing that no matter how bad it looks, God is in control. Just because it looks like the devil has the most points, don't believe for a minute that the devil wins. God will pull off the victory whenever He wants.

Just because the media doesn't discuss God's victories, He still wins. I think this is part of His strategy, too. If you think the devil is tricky, look how many people come to Christ with no media coverage.

When China was closed by the Communists, the number of Christians multiplied to around 50,000—that is by ten times! It is still happening in China, and now in many other countries too.

1. Who wins the war?

2. How can we speed up the conclusion of the war?

3. Who does God want to come into His Kingdom?

4. What kind of schedule is God on for the end of the Earth?

5. What is the war for anyway?

6. Is what God said to Joshua through Moses good for us?

7. What was God's recipe for success?

8. Look again at Joshua 1:5-9. How can you apply it to your own life at this time?

NOTES

Chapter 55

WHEN WILL THIS BATTLE BE OVER?

WE DON'T KNOW the date of Jesus' return. Only God knows, because He sees the end now. God inhabits eternity and in one glance sees the beginning, the end and everything in between. So who can outsmart Him? I'm a fan of God, and I like to be on the winning side.

God wants everybody to be saved from hell, so His mercy and grace still goes on. Because He knows how terrible hell is, he is not willing for any to perish and go there. He continues to wait and woo people, and if He wanted to He could say, "That's it. Sorry folks, we're done." I can't see Him doing that until He has given everyone everywhere the chance to be saved.

1. When did Jesus say the end will come?

2. Has everybody in the world heard the name of Jesus yet?

3. How did God make the battle possible for us?

4. What is Jesus waiting for before He can come back?

5. How does God want us to be involved in the Harvest?

6. With the devil stirring up disobedience and rebellion, how can God get man to cooperate?

7. The answer to the question of when the battle will be over is: when all have heard, and have the opportunity to choose to make Christ their Savior.

NOTES

Chapter 56

WE WIN!

THE OBJECT OF the race is to win. The object of the war is to win. God is doing His part in this spiritual warfare and we are doing our part. This is a winning combination for sure. The Holy Spirit says, "Go tell that person the Gospel." We obey and the Lord saves him. The Holy Spirit says, "Pray for that guy's healing." We pray and the Lord heals him. This is how we win the war. We cooperate with God and He does it.

The Lord's timing is perfect. The Lord is on His own timetable and not ours. I've heard an old saying that goes, "Pray like only the Lord can do it, and work like only we can do it." I think this is the recipe for victory.

1. In order to win a race, what preparations are necessary?

2. How do you practice for the race?

3. How do we prepare for the war and the victory?

4. Jesus, our leader and model, won. How did He win?

5. Who makes God's army so powerful it unnerves the enemy?

6. Even if some of the soldiers get wounded, do we still win?

7. One person alone can't win this war; it takes all of the army fighting shoulder to shoulder. But together, working with God, can we do it?

8. How can we tell the enemy is losing?

9. Who do we give the glory to for the victory?

NOTES

Chapter 57

PLUNDER THE DEVIL

ONE OF THE joys of battle is collecting the spoils. In this spiritual battle the spoils are people. It produces great joy when we see a slave of the devil get saved by the Prince of Peace, Jesus. We are happy for that person and the Kingdom of God. Then there comes more hard work. Even though there is a lot more work to be done, there's joy in the many little victories in the lives of those who are being discipled. These are "in your face" victories against the devil as that person grows in faith toward the Lord. These also equal plunder, and it's all good.

1. Now that the devil has been defeated by Jesus' death on the cross, how can we plunder the devil?

2. Do you think that many or a few will come into the Kingdom of God in the last days?

3. Jesus commands us to pray for laborers to go into the Harvest. Are we to be one of those harvesters we are praying for?

4. We are called to invite people to come to Jesus and to make them disciples. Most of us are better at one part or the other. Where do you see your part is in this process?

5. Are you willing to expand how you see your role and do both when needed?

NOTES

Chapter 58

THE VICTORY IS SWEET

ON EARTH, YOU train vigorously with high hopes of victory, and you end up winning. The hopes are not deferred but they are realized. All that work has paid off. Oh, what fun. This is like icing on the cake.

Only the worst grouch would not want the sweetness of victory. There are pictures of the streets of New York lined with smiling happy Americans greeting the military coming back from WW II. This victory made us happy, because we won and we no longer had to go to war. It was a sweet time for America.

1. The victory is sweeter than the battle is hard. What makes it so sweet?

2. It is good to see a person come into freedom, to come into a relationship with their Creator that will promise the benefits of the Kingdom now and Heaven after. Is that enough to convince them to get saved?

3. What holds people back from asking Jesus into their heart as their Lord and Savior?

4. Does the world's influence get a grip on some people?

5. What do we do to overcome people's fears and persuade them to come into God's Kingdom?

6. What person is not beautiful to the Lord Jesus?

7. How can people be helped to see through their confusion?

8. Would prayer for these people be the way for God to convince them they are valuable to Him?

NOTES

Chapter 59

EVERY SOLDIER NEEDS SOME R & R

NO MATTER WHAT kind of conflict there is, it is tiring. We say, "Can we take a break now?" Rest is good, especially in this relentless jungle-type warfare where you never know when or where the enemy will strike next. It will wear you down mentally, physically, and spiritually. Many can't take it. Only the Lord can help our soul, if we will let Him.

He also promises eternal rest, so that helps us keep going.

1. When does a soldier need rest?

2. How can we find rest in the battle?

3. We still need to fight every day, so when can we rest?

4. Can we appropriate God's peace, mercy, and grace daily?

5. Is there peace (rest) when we know God will turn all our adverse situations around for our good?

6. Can we rest in God's love?

7. How can we know we love God?

8. Can we get enough rest in the battle?

NOTES

Chapter 60

CUT OFF THOSE CURSES

MY WIFE, ROBERTA, told me that curses put heaviness on people that can and should be broken off in the Name of Jesus. These curses can be innocent negative words or complaints. Our words are powerful in the spirit realm. Whether our words are encouraging or discouraging they carry a certain amount of energy. We don't see what those words do all the time, but they are effective or affective. Words are powerful for hostility or for liberation. Choose them carefully.

1. Sometimes, through no fault of our own, people say negative things about us. Do we have the authority to cut off those curses and remove the power over us that they exert?

2. When Jesus forgave those that hung Him on the cross, He released them to be able to come into His Kingdom. Did some of them make it in?

3. In the spirit realm there is treachery afoot. Unbeknownst to the "curser" the enemy can make an end run with thoughts and words. What can the demons turn them into? Can we give the devil ideas on how to destroy someone? Recently I read a headline in the news where someone said that a person should just kill herself. Next thing you know, that is exactly what she had done. Could it be the demons used these attitudes and words as a curse to persuade her to destroy herself?

4. Do you think demons love negative words and works? What about rumors and gossip?

5. Is it more treacherous and fun if the person is innocent?

6. Will the devil make a case to break any Christian thrust against him?

7. What would be better to speak over a person than negative words?

NOTES

Chapter 61

THE ULTIMATE WEAPON IN SPIRITUAL WARFARE IS LOVE

THIS BOOK WAS not finished until I added this chapter on love. I knew something was missing, but couldn't figure it out for some time. The list of weapons in Ephesians doesn't detail love as a weapon. But as is common to the Bible, you have to put it all together to make a single teaching.

Somebody said that love is a spiritual weapon, and the bell went off in my head. That's it. I can finish the book now. I know there are more weapons that are a little less distinct that we need to know how to use, so we have to read the Bible again. What a wonderful book. I think that all the general questions are answered in the Bible.

I guess I'll have to read it again. I try to read it through at least once a year, because by the time I get to the New Testament the Old Testament principles are fuzzy again.

1. When there is war in the heavenly realm, how do we do war on Earth?

2. When we are loving people, are we going against the devil's plan?

3. Jesus died on the cross for our sins, so what do we do for others' sins?

4. How can love be such a powerful weapon?

5. How is love as a weapon both defensive and offensive?

6. How can anybody defend against this fruit of the Spirit?

7. What is the order of the day when we walk by the Spirit?

8. How can love fail?

9. Love triumphs first, last and always. Is there anything greater?

10. God is Love and He cannot fail.

NOTES

Contact Information

CPSIA information can be obtained
at www.ICGtesting.com
Printed in the USA
JSHW020333030421
13166JS00001B/4